THE METAL DETECTIVE

Treasures Lost and Friendships Found

To Marvin & Gloria
Hope you Enjoy

THE
METAL
DETECTIVE

Treasures Lost and

Friendships Found

By Alan Rothman

(edited by Jeffrey Neal Rothman)

Illustrations by Mark Gennaro

SMALL BATCH BOOKS

AMHERST, MASSACHUSETTS

Designed by Lisa Vega
Cover and interior illustrations by Mark Gennaro

ISBN 978-1-937650-60-5

Library of Congress Control Number: 2015945852

SMALL
BATCH
BOOKS

493 South Pleasant Street
Amherst, Massachusetts 01002
413.230.3943
smallbatchbooks.com

Special thanks to my grandchildren,
who appear on the back cover of this book. From left to right:
Owen, Cooper, Henry, Isaac, Emma, and Caroline.

CONTENTS

Prologue

"What's the best thing you've ever found?" It's the question people always ask as I scan the beach with my metal detector, a birthday gift from my kids a decade ago. And my answer is always the same: The instant kinship I've felt with complete strangers and the intriguing conversations I've had are rewards that surpass the thrill of discovering jewelry and coins buried beneath the sand. I've met so many kind, friendly people as I searched for treasures on beaches from Cape Cod to Hawaii. I never tire of sharing my stories with anyone who cares to listen. And in this book, I will share them with you.

*   *   *

The metal detector was a gift idea my kids had, so I would be occupied at the beach while my wife, Myrna, sat in her familiar spot at the water's edge. Initially, I thought such a hobby would be boring. I appreciated the thoughtfulness my kids put into the gift, but I was not excited about the prospect of walking up and down the beach waving with what people at first glance might think was a cane. When I finally decided to give it a try and immediately found my first coin, I was hooked. Now I'm grateful for the gift that never stops giving.

In my professional career as a certified public accountant (CPA), I'm responsible for making decisions that affect a client's financial future. It's a serious occupation; as a proverbial "bean counter," my clients put their faith in me to advise them wisely. My interaction with beachgoers is vastly different—the demeanor of those in the sun and at the ocean is relaxed and laid back.

Initially, my second career as a treasure hunter brought polite smiles from friends and family who likely thought I was going through a mid-life crisis. They probably thought to themselves, "What a dreamer that little guy is." Many years later, when I told these folks that I was planning on writing a book about my adventures with my metal detector, I received the same humoring looks.

The process of writing this book has been very exciting. I was surprised that the many non-believers in my family fired off suggestions as I worked through the writing. They were well intentioned, but I had to constantly remind them that the experiences were mine and that it was my turn to humor them!

Now, my dream has come true—I am able to share the wonderful experiences my hobby has given me. My hope is that there is a fellow dreamer out there who will follow in my footsteps after reading this book.

*   *   *

Special thanks to Myrna, who puts up with my hobby so patiently, and to all my children and grandchildren. Thanks also to the beachgoers, who made this book possible with their conversation and stories. Of course, I'm also thankful for the buried treasures left behind that have kept me excited all these years.

The collaboration with my son Jeff, who edited this book, is something that I will always remember fondly, forever locked up in my real treasure chest of memories.

—Alan Rothman

3

Liam's Glasses

A mother of a child who lost his prescription glasses politely asked me if I'd mind making a quick search on the beach with my detector. This simple request—and its outcome—compelled me to write this book.

My wife, Myrna, and I were staying at a Cape Cod resort. Liam (the boy who lost the glasses) and his family were vacationing at the same resort. Liam's mom told me that replacing her son's glasses would be expensive, and she would appreciate any effort on my part to locate her six-year-old's frames.

I searched for an hour with no luck. After the family packed up, I scanned my detector directly where they had been sitting. Remarkably, I found the glasses. I blared out my distinctive whistle—the one I always used to let my kids know dinner was ready. The family heard me and saw me waving my arms. Liam's mother was astonished when I handed her the glasses. She offered me free drinks at the bar, but I passed. I told her it was my pleasure to help her out. She thanked me and asked for my name and room number.

Half an hour later, there was a knock on my door. One of the hotel staff handed me an envelope containing a $50 gift certificate to the resort's restaurant with the following note attached:

"Al—thanks so much for finding Liam's glasses. Please have a bite of food on us."

That simple, meaningful act of kindness was a real case of paying it forward. I was honored by the sentiment. There would be more successful treasure hunts, some by request—as with Liam's mom—and others by plain old luck.

All-Inclusive Resorts

On several occasions I have traveled to "all-inclusive resorts" with my family and, of course, with my metal detector. Because guests have no need to bring money to the beach at these luxury hotspots, the quality "hits" I get are few and far between.

The majority of women wear fake jewelry, not wanting to risk traveling with their more valuable pieces. However, I do find the occasional, unusual coin from around the world, not just the U.S., which makes detecting at such beaches worthwhile.

Martin Van Buren even made an appearance by way of a 2008 commemorative $1 coin, surprising everyone in my family who witnessed the find. Even though the cost of a family trip runs into the thousands of dollars, finding that special coin made the sting to my bank account easier to handle—of course being with my family is also a pleasure.

One distinct advantage I have at these resorts is a real lack of competition from the locals, due to the fact that the islands I travel to are home to very few individuals who can afford to purchase a metal detector. Interestingly, at these resorts, I have also never seen another tourist with a metal detector, so I do attract a great deal of attention—which I never tire of.

The Pied Piper

There is a tangible curiosity among the beach crowd when I go to work with my detector; the younger set inevitably chase after me to see what I've found. I'm used to parents yelling at their kids as they rush toward me. To these kids I am a stranger, but their preoccupation with the loot I land challenges their common sense.

The Children's Beach on Nantucket requires pre-planning. I always ask Myrna to sit on a nearby bench. When nervous parents question my motives for attracting children, I wave to Myrna to assure them that I am legitimate. My new little friends tag along as we hunt for what I tell them are pirate treasures.

I enjoy my role as the Pied Piper, but the title presents unique challenges. The kids that follow me hope to witness the discovery of the fabled riches. Usually, a bevy of bottle caps turns up in the sand. The kids are amazed, though, when I do find a coin. Their looks of awe and wonder are heartwarming. Some ask if I've ever found a $100 bill with my detector, which always gives me a smile. Others point to areas they think are hot spots, as if they're equipped with X-ray vision—also good for a chuckle.

I am guilty of planting treasure for my grandchildren. They love to witness the find of a coin, or a Matchbox car, or really anything that isn't a bottle cap. Their attention span doesn't always allow for a lengthy search so the plant is a necessary offshoot of the hobby. I will, however, deny doing such a thing—until the grandkids are old enough to read this book.

My grandson Isaac often walks the beach with me. He is fascinated by dinosaurs and can recite the names and characteristics of the ancient creatures like a tiny, talking encyclopedia.

One summer day, with Isaac in tow, I dug my sifter in the sand after detecting a weak signal, only to come up empty. "False alarm," I said.

With a serious face and a look of amazement, he said, "A fossil arm! Wow, can I have it?!"

Determination & Patience

Considering my average day of metal detecting runs three hours, patience and a healthy dose of determination are required. The timing of the search is crucial; often I am weaving around beach blankets, chairs, and sand castles. Waiting for the beach to empty is not always possible.

However, the 95 percent success rate of finding something of value on my searches is reward enough for me—even if the amount of change I uncover often doesn't equate to minimum wage. Very few get rich with this hobby.

Some days I average 50¢ an hour. Replacing the two small batteries I need to power the detector can wipe out a week's profit. On the flip side, there are those precious few occasions where I earn in excess of $100 an hour when an expensive piece of jewelry is found.

Determination, or in my case, near obsession, will always fuel my desire to scour the beaches for treasure. I love the suspense and the mystery waiting to be uncovered. It's likely I will never tire of the hobby as long as it is physically possible for me to search.

I believe that at least one of my grandchildren will follow in my footsteps as a treasure hunter, and if they do, I will simply tell them, "Hey, I did that area already."

Abe Lincoln's Frown

Have you ever wondered why Abraham Lincoln bears a frown on his face on the penny? Can't blame him, because no one wants the coin he graces. I have great compassion and respect for the penny because it's the coin I most frequently find.

On many of my searches, a cluster of pennies will appear in the same area, as if they were tossed aside in one big handful. Since finding a quarter is rare, and may take up to one hundred hits to score, I appreciate the penny despite the general distaste with which it is regarded.

There are lessons to be learned from the penny. My neighbors' son, Max, has a December birthday, as do I. We usually exchange gifts. On his seventh birthday, I thought I would start him on the hobby of coin collecting. The penny seemed the logical choice— it's far less expensive than collecting vintage quarters.

On our way home from a coin shop, I told Max I was positive we could find pennies on the ground to add to his collection. He voiced his doubts, but quickly spotted four Lincolns as he scoured the ground, bumping into people along the way.

I like to believe that every child I've met on my treasure hunts will continue searching, as Max did that day. I will always be grateful to Abe Lincoln, not only for what he accomplished as president, but for the bountiful gifts he's given the metal detecting community . . . and my treasure chest.

Danger Danger

The dangers I've encountered with sharp and rusty discarded metal don't compare with what has transpired on Oak Island in Nova Scotia's Mahone Bay. Six people have lost their lives while searching for alleged buried treasure estimated to be worth millions of dollars. Then there are treasure hunters who concentrate on sunken ships, which present different, but equally life-threatening dangers.

The one time I feared for my safety was when I was hunting on what I thought was a deserted beach. I was surprised by a group of young people partying in the woods near where I was searching. There was a strong scent in the air and discarded bottles surrounding them. The apparent leader of the group approached me and asked if I could try to find his lighter. I accepted the challenge.

I found the lighter, much to my relief. I never told my wife and family about this adventure. Once again, my detector proved that it could be trusted to save the day.

Another party I happened upon was much tamer. A group of young people were spread out on beach blankets near an area where I had multiple hits. I found several coins and wondered where this honey hole came from.

I soon realized that the partying kids had seen me coming and planted my unexpected good fortune. I had a moral dilemma: Do I give back the coins and explain to them that this is not proper metal detecting etiquette? Or should I just pocket the coins? I'll let you guess what my final decision was.

Maui Adventures

Maui is a favorite vacation spot for me and Myrna. Don Nelson, the former Boston Celtic and the man who holds the record for most coaching wins in the NBA, is a very close friend and longtime client who lives in Maui with his wife, Joy, also a dear friend.

I have represented Don as his CPA since his professional playing days and deeply treasure his friendship. My tax practice has always specialized in handling pro athletes, but my relationship with Don is unique. We have a chemistry that balances both a business and personal connection. Don towers over me by more than a foot; "Mutt and Jeff" is the nickname that many of our friends have dubbed us when we are together. It was in Maui that Don pulled an epic metal detecting caper on me, but we'll get to that later in the book.

On one memorable day in Maui, I made the familiar sweep with my detector, waiting for the beep that signaled hidden treasure—or discarded beach junk. My kids could not have anticipated that gifting me the metal detector for my birthday would land me a twenty-year-old blonde as I ambled along the

Hawaiian coast. The thrill of the unknown—the secrets the sand clings to—always drove me, but that day in Maui was unique.

The beautiful girl approached me as I bagged a coin.

"Would you mind taking a picture with me?" she asked.

It was a puzzling request, the first of its kind. She explained that her father was a metal detecting enthusiast and a photo from Hawaii with a fellow treasure hunter would be appreciated.

I agreed, but only if she would do something for me. She eyed me with a wary look, as if I was going to ask for a favor she couldn't deliver.

"You see that woman sitting by the water's edge?" I pointed to my wife. "Would you come with me so I can show her what I found?"

The girl smiled and agreed.

"Hey, Myrna," I called, with the girl by my side. "Look what I found metal detecting!"

*   *   *

Hawaii was the setting for the strangest beach I've ever explored with my detector: a nude beach where I was the odd man out. I found very little on my hunt—understandable, since the beach-goers have no pockets for loose change. The coins I did find left me wondering where the person had carried their spare change—an exposed-fanny pack? Good grief!

*   *   *

"Who's this?" the caller asked.

"I'm the guy who found this phone in the sand," I replied.

This cell phone was the second I'd discovered in Hawaii. The caller couldn't believe the phone was still functioning and was very anxious to retrieve it. We set a place to meet and I gave him his phone—no reward except the satisfaction that I did a good deed. Note to reader: If you lose your cell phone at the beach, call your number from someone else's phone—I might just be the guy on the other end!

Fear of the Green Monster

During an extended stay at a resort, I heard a strange noise emanating from a nearby parking lot every morning at six a.m. My worst fear greeted me—a huge Green Monster was the source. The Monster's sole purpose was to rake the beaches clean of debris and anything else it could find—an absolute nightmare come to life.

I realized that the only way for me to defeat this beast was to wake up before it did—a strategy that couldn't go on indefinitely. I finally gathered up the nerve to approach the driver and voice my concerns that the monster would claim my potential treasures.

With a smile on his face, he said, "Take a good look, this baby can only rake up cans, dead horseshoe crabs, and other large items. So, you're safe!"

The Green Monster was not the threat I had assumed, and in a strange way, I became somewhat attached to the big guy for the rest of my stay.

Barber Cut

Hawaii and Cape Cod are not the only locales I have scoured. The beaches in South Boston, minutes from my home, yielded my oldest coin: a "Barber" dime from the late 1800s. The coin was in poor condition, but I knew there had to be some value. A young girl approached me after I pocketed the dime.

As most youngsters do, she asked me if I had found anything worthwhile. I proudly produced the Barber. The girl said her parents owned an antique shop and might be able to pin down the coin's worth. She waved her mom over; I held my breath—nervous anticipation circling my stomach.

"What do you do with your treasures?" the woman asked.

"I keep them in a treasure chest."

In a serious, hushed tone, she dropped a bombshell: "What would you do if the item was worth $20,000?"

I swallowed hard and called Myrna to tell her that I had possibly hit the "mother lode." I rushed home, turned on my computer, and surfed the net. Due to its condition, the coin was only worth $1.45. The antique shop owner had had her fun with me, but for those forty-five minutes between the find and the disappointing conclusion of my research, I was riding high.

It was years later that I did indeed find a mother lode . . . .

Fool's Gold

I t always amazes me when people choose to wear expensive jewelry to the beach rather than leave the valuables at home or, if on vacation, in a hotel safe.

An elderly woman I encountered lost a very expensive gold earring that was one of a pair her husband had given her as an anniversary present. I told her that the odds of me finding it were extremely slim.

I spent an hour searching for the earring. It wasn't until I had given up and was demonstrating to her how I sweep an area (with the detector turned off) that the earring appeared at our feet! Sheer luck, but even in the off position, my detector came through.

*　　*　　*

A long shot in metal detecting is finding a pair of matching earrings. In fact, it's nearly impossible. It's unusual for a woman to lose both at the beach. I found a nice earring on one of my hunts and showed it to Myrna, hoping that it was something of real value. She said it was—only if I found the matching one.

I walked away discouraged. I returned to searching the beach and heard that familiar ping. There it was—the matching earring! The pair now sits in my wife's jewelry box.

*   *   *

Do I feel obligated to find the owner of a piece of jewelry I discover? I'm often asked this question.

Most of my discoveries are made on public beaches. As a result, identifying the owner is nearly impossible unless the piece of jewelry has distinctive marks indicating who its owner might be. If I find an item of significant value on a resort beach, I leave my contact information in case the owner comes forward.

I've read many articles of wedding and graduation rings and other jewelry being returned to their rightful owners after being discovered several years after their loss. Although this has never happened to me, I look forward to the day I could be an integral part of such a reunion.

*   *   *

I do have difficulty distinguishing the jewels from the fakes. That's strictly Myrna's job. Most of the stones that I've been certain were diamonds have not been the real deal. As with the Barber dime, the elation of the moment, the adrenaline that surges through me when I think I've hit something big, is sure to sink when my finds turn out to be inauthentic. One particular ring appeared to have multiple diamonds, but Myrna can spot a fake from twenty yards away. She said it was just for show and probably worth $50, not $5,000. Still, the searches continue.

A House Saved

The water damage to my Cape Cod home was so extensive that I thought I might lose it. Ironically, it was a metal detector that saved my house.

It was mid-January when I went to check on the house—a necessary task in the winter months. Inside, water poured out of the walls and ceilings—the result of breaks in pipes that had frozen. This particular winter in the Northeast was marked by consecutive days of frigid temperatures along with power loss. A disaster was well under way by the time I arrived.

The basement had six feet of water; more than 23,000 gallons had come through the pipes. The fire and police departments came to the immediate conclusion that this was an emergency water situation.

To my surprise, the water department emergency team arrived with metal detectors—an absolute must for locating the street-level shut-off valve under a heavy layer of snow. Although the team had a general idea of the valve's location, without metal detectors, valuable time would be lost in saving a home.

The detectors saved me hundreds of thousands of dollars and

made me realize how many important and varied uses this invention offers, apart from just being a hobby for treasure seekers. I will forever be grateful for that day in January when my house was saved by a metal detector.

Withdrawal Pains

Living in the Northeast certainly limits the months that are conducive to metal detecting. My search for treasure begins in early May and continues into late October, after which point the withdrawal pains strike.

Occasional trips to warmer climates in the winter months allow me to continue my hobby sporadically. I do wonder if, given the opportunity, I would be physically able to metal detect twelve months a year; constantly bending over to scoop the sand can be exhausting. Some people might question how treasure hunting is physically demanding, but, as I mentioned, the three hours a day I average on my searches—sometimes in unpleasant conditions—is not for everyone. On most occasions, I can accept the challenges of the weather conditions—wind, broiling sun, and rain—but, unlike the mailman, I don't venture out in blinding snow and freezing temperatures.

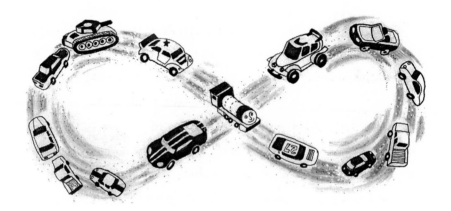

Sinker Stinkers & Other Nuisances

For the three hours of metal detecting I average in a day, I get 300 to 500 hits. Of those pings, less than 5 percent have any value; the rest is basically trash. Unfortunately, offending items of the same kind of junk repeatedly worm their way into my sifter.

Fishing sinkers are one of those constants, especially near jetties. Fishermen lose these like kids lose their toy cars in the sand. The frustrations of my hobby are not limited to disappointing sinkers. I've found endless bottle caps (I gave up counting at 3,000), 1,000 hairpins (my wife refuses to use them), a myriad of soda can flip tops, and 123 dead batteries (or was it 124?).

The most unusual unwanted find was close to a hundred used shell casings. As I sifted through the casings, I hoped that the shooter was done and a duck-and-run from stray bullets would not be necessary.

The sheer volume of junk is amazing—it's incredible that so many people feel that burying their trash on the beach is acceptable. I guess the beach crowd doesn't realize that treasure hunters are lurking. July 5th is easily the most dreadful day to look for loot. The metal in the fireworks used the previous night wreak havoc on a search.

I hang on to dangerous items that find their way into my sifter and dispose of them. I feel a duty to rid the beach of as many pieces of jagged metal, fishing hooks, and other dangers as I can—it's an unspoken obligation.

The guilt I feel associated with leaving some of the trash behind has always bothered me, but it would be extremely difficult to cart away the bulk of the junk. When small children follow me, I take the time to explain to them that using a sifter is much safer than digging in the sand with their hands. The garbage is a nuisance for metal detectors, but when I find something precious, in that less-than-5-percent category, I'm compelled to fight another day.

Hall of Fame?

Don invited me to attend his induction ceremony to the prestigious NBA Hall of Fame, and now I can't help but wonder if I will ever be able to enjoy the same honor in the Treasure Hunter's Hall of Fame, if such a place is ever built.

Though it may be hard to believe, after doing some research, I've found there are metal detecting clubs that have instituted their own halls of fame. If a national hall is established, I envision the day may come when I receive a call or letter informing me that I will be recognized as the first inductee for my persistence in chasing the dream.

For the time being, I will have to be satisfied with the treasures I find—and hope the fame comes at a later date.

Just the Facts

I operate a car dealership in my garage—not the kind of cars that can be driven, but miniature toys I've found. My grandchildren drool at the array of cars and trucks I have accumulated, but don't understand the meaning of an inheritence—that's when I will pass along my finds. Until then, hands off!

*   *   *

Car keys, house keys, and hotel room keys—I've found quite a few. I can only imagine a beachgoer's stress in returning to their car only to find they've lost their keys. On one occasion, strangely enough, after finding an ordinary key, I was shocked to happen upon the matching padlock.

*   *   *

I enjoy putting a competitive spin on my hunts. One of the holy grail discoveries I look forward to is the four-coin-scoop—a rarity I've struck only twice in the many thousands of finds I've made. It's incredibly exciting to reach down and find more than one coin in my sifter.

*　　*　　*

There is often stiff competition when I set out to explore a beach. Considering the average age of my fellow treasure seekers is seventy-five, being stiff is not surprising!

No set rules exist for multiple detectives occupying the same area. It's every man for himself. Most of us stretch the truth and tell each other there's not much to find—hoping to discourage the hunter from continuing his pursuit.

*　　*　　*

With the exception of trips to Cuba and Europe, I always take my trusted detector with me. It seems strange to me that the airport's metal detector has never been a problem for me. Must be a professional courtesy among the tightly knit group of electronics.

*　　*　　*

One of the strangest finds I hit upon was a pen—not because there was anything unusual about the pen, but because the circumstances surrounding the find were.

Myrna and I were at the beach, settling in for a pleasant afternoon. Myrna works in real estate and is in constant communication with her clientele. She takes notes while she works, but on this particular day, she left home without a pen. She asked me if I had one with me, which I didn't. Within minutes of my metal detecting routine, I found a working pen! We thought how coincidental it was that the very thing we needed at that moment was buried right in front of us.

* * *

My twelve-year-old granddaughter Emma, being the trooper that she is, accompanied me one summer day in detecting for hours. We found the usual junk: fishing hooks, empty soda cans, a few butter knives and forks. Emma's day with me paid off though. I found a Tiffany charm with the engraved words, "I Love You" on it, which I gave to her. In this case, she didn't have to wait for her inheritance.

* * *

Speaking of soda cans, I now realize that recycling the cans at 5¢ apiece would have earned me a pretty penny. However, one should never look back, only forward, while metal detecting (pun intended).

Foreign Exchange

Air travel has allowed me to expand my search for treasure to distant resorts. I have found coins from several countries, lost by travelers from around the world who take their money to the beach instead of leaving it in their hotel room safe.

The Euro is especially valuable when compared to U.S. coins, and is therefore a welcome addition to my treasure chest. I do extensive research on foreign coins when I find them to determine their value. Much to my surprise, I once located a coin with a value of $5, making that a memorable day of detecting.

Some foreign coins, like stamps, are more elaborately detailed when compared to their U.S. counterparts. I imagine that in the early days of metal detecting, finding a foreign coin must have been a rarity. For this, I am forever grateful to the Wright brothers.

An Olympic Run

I have been an addicted runner for more years than I can remember. The combination of that habit with my metal detecting hobby puts me in top physical shape for an Olympic competition—that is, if the union of the two were to be established as an Olympic sport. Of course, the winners would receive gold, silver, and bronze coins instead of medals.

Imagine individuals from every country competing in the Sahara desert in search of treasure! Metal detecting is not for the weak of mind or body; competitors would spend hour after hour baking in the hot sun, constantly bending over and performing the most difficult maneuver—waving the arm back and forth over the ground.

No one should underestimate the difficulty of holding the detector and sweeping it across the sand in a controlled manner. It's not that easy. I'm sure my doctors are quite amazed at the strength I have in that arm. These same doctors seek to help in any way they can with constant reminders to wear a hat and use sunscreen—how great is that?

Keeps on Ticking

"If you find a Rolex, it's mine."

The strategy of some adults to claim the rights to any Rolex watches I may find is just good-natured fun. I have found several watches over the years, but none functioned—except one. I was astounded by just how well this particular watch works.

But despite how well the watch functions, I haven't managed to give it away. I offered it to my wife, who promptly dismissed me. Next in line for the watch was my granddaughter Emma who politely declined. I was shocked that she turned her grandfather down. Lastly, a housekeeper at a resort Myrna and I stayed at responded in broken English that she didn't want it.

I admit that it's not the Rolex I've chased after; I know it's just a simple, cheap $14.95 timepiece, and I know it will likely be displayed in my treasure chest for future generations to reject, but it will forever be my John Cameron Swayze watch (it keeps on ticking). For those of the younger generation, your elders can acquaint you with this Mr. Swayze.

The Elusive Silver Dollar

Writing is much more grueling than I anticipated. During one stretch of composing this
book, I took a break and did the most relaxing
thing I could think of—metal detecting, of course.

I took off for the beach where I found the usual toy car and
was fairly content with that until my sensor rang out a strong
signal. I had never found as much as a whole dollar with a single
scoop, but on this day that changed.

There in my sifter was an Eisenhower silver dollar, not the
usual sand dollar that one finds on the shores, but a real trophy.
This is a treasure that I will credit my book for helping me discover; I will always remember the day fondly.

Now, when it comes to presidents, Eisenhower is certainly
preferred over Lincoln!

Lifeguard on Duty

The lifeguards I encounter at the beach are always friendly and respectful as I weave my way through the masses soaking up the sun. It is taboo to set up a beach blanket in front of the lifeguard stand, as it could inhibit the guard from running to an ocean emergency, but scanning the area with my detector is fine unless such an emergency is unfolding.

The politeness of the lifeguards towards me could be due to the fact that most are a third of my age and they are simply respecting me as an elder. I make a point of greeting them and I hand over dangerous items that could harm a beachgoer— knives with open blades, shell casings, fingernail clippers, or used needles.

On one occasion, a lifeguard at the National Seashore on Cape Cod asked me if I could help him find his lost gold ring. Unfortunately, I had to remind him that this particular beach was off-limits to detectors; the fear being that digging in the sand would have an adverse effect on the beach's appearance. The life-guard approached me because my detector was lying beside me on my blanket, even though I couldn't use it. I always keep my trusted friend with me in case I pass a beach, and on this day, I didn't want to leave it exposed in the car.

Rarely, if ever, is a seasoned metal detective enjoying the sun without firing up his machine. As I've always said, there is no rest for the weary when treasure is waiting to be found.

Brian

The young man had a simple request. He asked that I try to find a watch he lost on a town beach in Nantucket. Brian, who was in his early twenties, was very emotional as he told me the story behind the watch. He explained that his late grandmother gave matching watches to Brian and his brother, who had passed away. Since losing his own watch a while back, Brian had worn his brother's as a reminder of him. That watch, too, was now gone.

The town beach where Brian believed he lost his brother's watch was five miles from where I was working my detector. He pleaded with me to pack up and try to find the missing watch. I explained that my wife was with me and I couldn't just leave her behind.

Brian insisted on calling Myrna, leaving a voicemail that I believe she still has in her phone: "Hi, this is Brian," he said. "I just met your husband, Al, who wants to know if it would be ok to leave with me and go into town to find my watch."

Myrna called back quickly and suggested that the three of us should leave immediately to begin the search. Time is always of the essence on a treasure hunt. Shifting sands and pounding feet can bury an item and make the search more difficult.

Unfortunately, the area of the beach where Brian suspected he lost the watch was a boat launching area and the sand was filled with nails, chains, and other junk—not conducive to metal detecting, and we were ultimately unsuccesful. But Brian was very appreciative of my effort and felt in a strange way comforted that he had done all he could to find the watch. He seemed at peace, and told us he would recount the story of our search to his family and try to find an exact replacement.

Karma? I have my doubts about this philosophy, but after Brian left, on another area of the same beach, I found a silver bracelet. It does make you wonder . . . .

Like a Fish Out of Water

On the rare occasions I find myself at the seashore without my detector, I feel like a fish out of water. Metal detecting is now part of my DNA makeup. I try to avoid trips to the beach without my detector, but that circumstance arises from time to time when I take my family to a restaurant on the water's edge after a long road trip.

I really don't even want to look at the beach; I feel helpless without my trusty friend. Words fail me to describe my reaction when I see a fellow treasure hunter, especially when he scoops anything up—even a rusty bottle cap!

My detector has become an integral part of my being—it is an extended member of my family. Unfortunately, there are times when it is impractical to have it with me.

A trip to Cuba caused me incredible anxiety. It's a country with beautiful, pristine beaches with strict regulations for foreigners—they would surely not look the other way if I attempted to bring in my metal detector. I had withdrawal pains throughout that trip, especially when we had beachfront meals and visited cultural beachside exhibits.

I am positive that no one in my group of travelers realized that they were in the company of someone who needed an intervention for emotional stress resulting from an addiction to treasure hunting.

I can only imagine the panic I'd feel if I were ever stranded on a deserted island with my detector and dead batteries. Now that's a nightmare!

Marriage

Are there negative aspects to my hobby? I cannot count the times that Myrna has scolded me for tracking in sand on recently cleaned floors. Another recurring egregious felony of mine is dumping sand into our washing machine from the pile that sits in my pockets after a day of detecting. The solution to the sand pile would be to carry a pouch for my loot during searches, but I insist on being a minimalist when I scour the beach.

The day I lost track of time—spending many more hours detecting than I usually allot—left Myrna in a fit of worry. She was sure that I was hospitalized somewhere from excessive sun exposure.

My addiction to this hobby is the cause for constant battles between Myrna and me. Should I please my wife or hunt for treasure? The debate between us ended one magnificent day . . . but I'll wait until the end of the book to tell you why.

My Dilemma

The biggest dilemma that looms regarding my hobby is what will become of all my loot? I am very protective of every coin, miniature car, key, and even piece of fake jewelry I find. When one of my grandchildren asks for something from my collection, I cringe.

As I mentioned earlier, I take enormous pride in giving good advice to clients in my role as a CPA in the area of financial planning and protection of their wealth. I am simply practicing what I preach.

Deciding what to do with my treasures when, at last, I must give them up is agonizing. I could leave it all to my grandchildren; I'm sure Myrna wouldn't want the tonnage of sandy coins, costume jewelry, and rusty fishing hooks. I have considered burying my finds with me, but I'm fearful that another treasure hunter will find my stash.

As of this writing, I am still contemplating the final resting place for my collection . . . .

Family Ties

I have always considered myself a devoted husband (fifty years and counting) and family man, aiming to be there for my children in their time of need. However, I have to admit that when the moment arises on the beach when I have to choose between my beloved hobby and my family, treasure hunting usually takes priority.

The first instance of me abandoning my family occurred on a beach trip in 2003. Of course, I brought my new metal detector with me. No sooner did we arrive than I had the urge to depart from my loved ones and start my search for gold. Since that fateful day, I no longer bring a beach chair for myself and instead take my guilty conscience with me in its place.

I have been known to leave elderly bus riders standing so that my trusty friend and I can have a safe place to sit (Nantucket Surf Side Beach has bus access). Am I a bad person because of my addiction to metal detecting? My guilt is somewhat alleviated when my grandchildren accompany me in my search for pirates' treasures.

My favorite metal detecting proverb is "time is money," similar to the one I share with my grandchildren on Halloween—"time is candy." I cannot imagine simply sitting on a beach with my family while treasures await me. Thus, I will forever be torn between being with my family and hitting the sand with my faithful metal detector.

On Call

A resort conglomerate approached me to be "on call" for the purpose of locating items that were lost by their guests. This opportunity comes up quite frequently. The going rate is $25 an hour, which is the responsibility of the guest. The thought of being paid is intriguing, not just because of the hourly rate, but also due to the fact that anything I find, other than the lost item, is mine to keep.

My mother had always hoped that I would become a doctor. Being an on-call detective is the next best profession. Although an attractive and enticing proposition, the idea of receiving calls and being available at a moment's notice may offset the advantages.

The emotions I've enjoyed upon returning a lost item, as in the case with Liam's glasses, is incredibly rewarding. Being compensated by the hour would be a very different experience than my usual treasure hunts.

Can my metal detecting be a business? Or only a hobby? Or can it be both?

For now, I am struggling with my decision and have not yet made a commitment to the resort owners. Maybe they can sweeten the pot by offering me vacation time. It doesn't hurt to ask.

One if by Land . . .

Metal detecting is not limited to the beach. There are brave souls who battle the ocean's waves to treasure hunt. More than a few times I have observed what appeared to be a Navy Seal fighting the surf, only to realize it was a comrade searching the ocean floor for valuables.

The underwater route requires a headset and a sifter attached to a long pole. The theory is that swimmers lose jewelry in the water just as they do on the beach. The competition in the water is far less intense than for the rest of us on dry land.

Those who choose this route have told me that the search can be very rewarding, but the hits are far fewer. I am strictly a land-lubber, a desert trooper walking for endless hours, dehydrated and nursing an aching back from repetitive bending. I always enjoy the camaraderie I feel with beachgoers, but those who choose to take their detectors into the tide are far more isolated.

Still other folks concentrate on older buildings, former mining land, fields, and abandoned property. In September of 2009, one of the most significant finds was unearthed in a rural field outside of London: more than 500 pieces of a seventh-century Anglo-Saxon hoard worth millions of dollars.

Other notable field finds include an antique Model T Ford that was buried intact for future generations to discover, as well as stolen coins that a postal worker grabbed, and other unusual treasures. One day, I might just pass by a field or an old building and take the opportunity to try my luck with this change of venue. Digging in the dirt is something my mother told me never to do, but if I were to uncover riches, I'm sure she'd have no complaints.

Pocketing the Goods

Metal detecting can often produce strange reactions. When I'm on a beach crowded with sunbathers, most will ignore me until my detector emits that shrill sound of a hit. All eyes are on me then, only some discreetly, as I dig for my find.

My first reaction is to avoid eye contact with anyone, unless the discovery is a bottle cap or other form of trash, which I will quickly show to those who are interested. However, even it's just a penny I uncover, I quickly put it in my pocket and let them wonder what I've found.

Always, if I'm asked, I will show off the new buried treasure, but I really like to keep people guessing. I'm not entirely sure why I react this way; maybe I want them to think I found a missing Rolex or that gold coin that everyone likes to ask about.

During one of my searches at a beach resort, a wedding was taking place on the lawn directly above me. It was a sunset wedding and I was alone on the beach. The guests and bride and groom were absorbed in the moment—until I came along. For one brief moment, I'd swear the focus was on me. I couldn't help but think of how many carats the bride's diamond might weigh, and what the odds were that she could lose it!

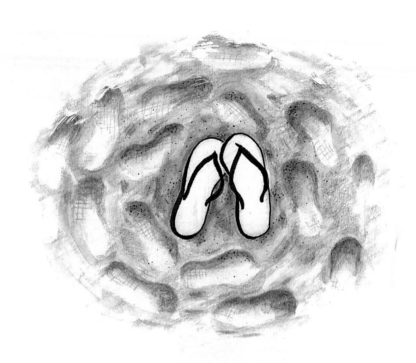

Skillfully Lucky

I'd like to think that experience has served me well in the years I've been metal detecting, but a bit of luck always helps. Luck—even a matter of a few inches—can mean the difference between finding gold and uncovering a bottle cap.

My experience leads me to locations similar to where I've had previous success; playgrounds and volleyball courts are favorites. I take special care around such places before heading off to other areas of the beach. I estimate that of my finds, approximately 50 percent consist of multiple coins found in the same spot.

I constantly question myself when I walk across the beach—should I move a bit to the left or the right? It's helpful to wear flip flops or sneakers, which leave imprints that prevent, to a certain extent, repetitive detecting over an area.

There is an old saying in metal detecting: "If the shoe doesn't fit, don't quit." Luck has certainly been on my side over my detecting career, but I like to think that experience has had a hand in my success as well.

Professional Ethics

I think it's safe to assume that many of my readers will either be current or former clients of my tax practice. I have always counseled my clients on the need to report all their taxable income on their returns; now I face an ethical decision regarding the contents of my treasure chest.

I read in the news about a couple who discovered a cache of coins valued at more than $10 million while walking their property and, much to their surprise, may face a sizeable tax liability when the coins are eventually sold.

So here's my dilemma: I could go to the local supermarket and cash in my coins in an automated machine—if the coins would be accepted with the sand still attached. No one would know how much I've collected, but will I feel guilty if I don't declare the cash?

The possibility that someone who reads my book could be an IRS agent or a former disgruntled client will sway my answer to yes! I will either declare the proceeds or go back to the beach and systematically bury the treasure over miles of sand.

Let this be a lesson to my children and grandchildren: Do the right thing!

Searching for Treasures by Gender

The definition of treasure hunting is quite different for women and men. I have never seen a female metal detective in all my years of experience. I've attributed that to the physical demands of the hobby.

However, I have now come to realize that women may have, in fact, much *more* patience, drive, and stamina in their search for treasures—except their venues are department stores, not the seashore.

Go shoe shopping with a woman and you will see it takes just as much (or more) patience as detecting. One reason women likely steer clear of metal detecting is not only to avoid finding rusty nails, but perhaps to avoid chipping their own nails!

On a more serious note, I am sure that one day I will meet a fellow detective of the opposite sex. I will be the first to wish her good luck in her quest for treasures.

Surprise, Surprise

A distraught woman on a crowded Nantucket beach made a beeline for me during one of my many trips to the island. Her husband had lost his wedding band the day before. Finding a specific small item is always a long shot, but I never refuse.

The hunt was on.

The distressed woman said that the ring had engraved initials—always a key detail if others try to claim ownership after a find. I came up empty in my hour-long search and apologized; frustrated and beaten by the sand.

Three football fields away from the area I just searched, a mother asked if I could show her children how my detector works. She buried a butter knife, and the kids marveled as the distinct shrill of my machine rang out. She asked me what I enjoyed most about the hobby, aside from the obvious thrill of finding jewelry and coins. I told her that meeting so many nice, inquisitive people was my greatest reward. I also mentioned that someone had just asked me to find a lost wedding band.

"Hey, mister, I found a ring yesterday," a teenage boy said.

He was lying on a blanket nearby and overheard our conversation. I asked him if he had given the ring to a lifeguard. He said he hadn't, and graciously offered to give up the ring if the initials matched the lost wedding band. Amazingly, it was the missing ring. The boy and I walked the beach and found the grieving woman. What a thrill it was to hand her the ring.

"You found it!" she said to me.

"Well, sort of. . . . "

The Bottle-Cap
Conundrum

My attitude regarding bottle caps has always been the same: They are a nuisance and a hindrance to a successful treasure hunt. At times, I have scolded my young followers when they attempt to pocket the bottle caps that my sifter captures in its clutches.

"Don't even think about taking that rusty old cap back to your parents," is my usual comment.

While writing this book, I began to wonder if it was possible that somewhere there are people who treat the bottle caps as treasures. Much to my surprise, I discovered that there are in fact many clubs, both local and international, that collect my nemesis.

Did I miss the boat?

My cap is off to these unique individuals. The first chance I get I will go to the nearest dumpster and send them whatever bottle caps I find. For that matter, I'll send along empty bottles as well, as long as the five-cent deposit is returned to me.

In the Black

"Has your metal detector paid for itself?" This is another question I'm frequently asked. My answer is always the same: I've been in the black since I found my first penny. My children's generous gift allowed me to reap an immediate profit with my second "career." The unit retails for about $150 and has brought me treasures in the thousands of dollars.

Metal detectors range from the very simple to the highly sophisticated. Some detectors are as pricey as $3,000; others are waterproof and require headsets. The perforated sifter I use to scoop up my finds can run between $20 and $25. There are two types available: a hand held, and one with an attached pole to avoid bending over.

In general, I have discouraged parents from buying a detector for children ten years or younger because most quality machines are too heavy for a child to handle comfortably. Searches also require infinite patience—a trait that children usually don't have, especially while lugging around a heavy detector.

A children's version is really a toy with minimal capabilities of making finds and will likely frustrate the child. Despite repeated requests, I have never allowed a kid to use my detector—the thought of my precious machine falling into little, foreign hands makes me shudder.

Fascination With the Seashore

The public's fascination with and love of the seashore is the driving force that makes my hobby worthwhile. Watching the ebb and flow of the ocean's tide and worshiping the sun are what draw most people to the beach. I don't take the environment for granted, even though most of my time searching for treasures is spent looking down at the sand, trying to avoid beach chairs and other obstacles.

I do take the time to marvel at the beauty of the ocean and the pleasure it brings. My other pastime, boating, provided many enjoyable years; my decision to give it up recently was made easier when I realized it would free up more time for metal detecting.

There is an old saying that the two happiest days of owning a boat are the day you buy it and the day you sell it. I never look back with regret that I sold my boat, but I sometimes find myself gazing at the boats on the water while detecting. When I happen upon a coin, though, I think of how much better it feels than filling up a bottomless gas tank!

Don Nelson's Flagrant Foul

I often travel to Maui to visit my close friends and clients, Don Nelson, and his wife, Joy. When Don's seventieth birthday was approaching, his family asked me if I thought a metal detector might be a good gift for a man who really seemed to have everything a person could want. I agreed and assisted in choosing a detector that would best suit Don. It was promptly ordered.

I visited Don shortly after his birthday and suggested that we go detecting together—a move that set into motion a devious plan. This was the first time Don had done any serious metal detecting. He wasn't sure where he had left his detector, but after some rummaging around, he found it, dusted off the cobwebs, and off we went.

Within a relatively brief period of time, we discovered three beautiful ornate glass eggs buried with their metal stands. We also found expensive jewelry in the same area. I looked at Don in amazement. "Do you have any idea how long I have searched for treasures like these?!"

He maintained a serious look. We both came to the conclusion that what we found must be items buried by a thief who would return after dark. That night, Myrna agonized over how we could split up the three eggs and which one she wanted. We made the decision that since we were guests of Don and Joy, they would have first dibs on the goods.

The next day, we broke out the detectors again and as we walked, Don encountered many friends who smiled at us and probably wondered if Don had lost all the money he made as a ballplayer and coach and now had to resort to metal detecting with me. Once again, we found a treasure trove of jewelry. I chalked it up to beginner's luck for Don.

There is an antique store across from Don's home. I took the liberty of bringing some of our finds to the place to be appraised. A young man offered me $50 for a silver bracelet. I almost sold the piece, but explained that my detecting partner had to approve since we were splitting the booty equally. If he agreed, I said, then I would come back to make the sale.

I was so excited that I could hardly wait to tell Myrna, Don, and Joy of our possible impending sale. We were all enjoying the moment. It was getting late and Don asked me to put off the sale until the next day and relax in the Jacuzzi, which I agreed sounded like a good idea.

There we were, Don smoking his cigar and me basking in the thought of finally finding that pot of gold I had looked so hard for. Don started telling me a story of when he was a rookie in the NBA. It was standard practice for the players to play tricks on the new members of the team and on the coaches.

He asked me if anyone had ever fooled me and of course, me

being a seasoned professional and very astute, I told him confidently, no way could I be so gullible to be fooled by anyone. He looked at me strangely and said he had once played a trick on me. Unable to recall any pranks, I asked what the trick was. He proceeded to tell me that he had planted all of our finds prior to us going out metal detecting for the last two days, and that all of the jewelry and other expensive items were Joy's!

It turns out that the silver bracelet I debated selling for $50 was worth a whole lot more than that. My only regret to this day is that I wish I had caught on to the trick so I could pretend to have sold everything to someone on the street for $100. That would have upset Don and Joy, but at least I would have had the last laugh! Still, the four of us always remember that time fondly, and whenever the story is recounted, it puts a smile on everyone's face.

A Penny for Your Thoughts

Although I have spent my entire adult life accounting for and managing millions of dollars as a CPA, I am more fascinated with the pocket change I've found. I can honestly say that, over the years, I've saved my clients hundreds of thousands of dollars, possibly millions, in tax savings, but it doesn't compare to finding as little as $1.50 while metal detecting. I am beginning to wonder where my priorities are!

Age has a lot to do with it; as I've gotten older, the simpler things in life have taken on greater significance. I thank my late father, Sam, for the value I put on saving a dollar; it is in my genes. My dad was a self-made man who paved the way for my profession in accounting. I have very fond memories of the times we spent together as father and son and as business partners in our accounting firm. Dad would be proud of my treasure chest of finds and likely encourage me to keep on searching.

Saying Goodbye to an Old Friend

We have all experienced having to say goodbye to an old friend. My trusty and rusty metal detector is getting tired, occasionally sending false signals—a sign of the aging process.

My friend has been by my side for more than a decade and has given me great pleasure as we searched for treasure on numerous beaches. Some might ask, "How can you get attached to a piece of metal?" As I said earlier, it's simply a gift that keeps on giving—gold earrings, watches, bracelets, and other jewelry have been scooped up on our travels together. What better gift than the gift of gold?

Myrna has been pleading with me for the past few years to accept a new detector for my birthday. I have been tempted to take her up on offer, but refuse to abandon my little buddy. It is true the more sophisticated metal detectors can actually determine what is under the surface and would save me a great deal of time and effort. I would no longer have to scoop up useless, discarded items.

I will likely pass my friend on to one of my grandchildren.

In this way, it will always be a part of my family. On my next birthday, I may surprise Myrna by accepting a gift of a new detector (hint, hint). Regardless, treasure awaits me—whether I move on to a new piece of equipment or stick with the tried and true.

The Second Best Thing
I've Ever Found

My family, especially Myrna, never really took me seriously in the early stages of my hobby. For the most part, they didn't encourage or discourage me on my daily trips to hunt for the pot of gold that waits at the end of the rainbow.

In some respects I became a source of entertainment for them. I thought, and hoped, that someday I would prove to them all that metal detecting was serious business!

It was a hot Fourth of July when I ventured off to search for treasures, leaving my family at home to enjoy the day by the pool. It was fairly late in the afternoon with the wind blowing briskly and the sand swirling—not ideal conditions for sunbathing at the beach or for metal detecting.

In the first hour, I had found less than a dollar's worth of change, until again my detector rang out, and a six-inch scoop uncovered the best thing I've ever found, besides friends: a diamond bracelet with three carats' worth of diamonds beautifully laid in eighteen-karat marked gold. The piece had a total of 110 tiny, glistening diamonds.

The public beach was empty as I put the bracelet gently in my pocket and swiftly walked the mile back to my house. My family greeted me with the usual, "So how many pennies did you find today?"

I asked my wife, "What are the two things you hope I find someday for you?"

She responded, "Diamonds and gold," as I handed her the bracelet. She screamed, "It is so beautiful. I love it!"

Her reaction confirmed that the piece was very valuable. The next decision was what to do with this great piece of jewelry. We went to a local jeweler to get a quick appraisal. He offered me $700 on the spot. By the look he gave me, I knew that we needed to take the bracelet to my wife's long-time Boston jeweler to get a true valuation.

My family was completely shocked when we told them that Myrna's friend told us to get the bracelet insured for $7,000!

The bracelet now belongs to Myrna. The good news is I found a rare, wonderful treasure; the bad news is my wife kept it. On a positive note, I am no longer made fun of and Myrna very willingly packs lunches for my trips to the beach, hoping to add to her jewelry box.

Will I ever discover a more valuable piece? One never knows. The fun is in the challenge, not necessarily the results.

Oh, by the way, Mr. Nelson, I got the last laugh!

Epilogue

When I began writing this book I never imagined how much laughter and how many smiles it would bring to my family and friends as I read portions of my work in progress to them. The book became a common thread that frequently came up in conversation. It's been a unique experience to be able to share the beginning of a new "chapter" in my life.

The reactions from my youngest grandchild to my ninety-six-year-old mother were the very same: laughter, smiles, and encouragement to continue reading more of the book to them.

For some reason, just the mention of metal detecting injects levity into a conversation. I truly believe that there is a potential book in everyone, just as everyone has a hobby or interest that brings them joy. In my case, it has been such a joy to be able to share my love for this hobby. Special thanks to all those individuals young and old who helped me by simply saying, "Go for the gold and finish it already."

Alan Rothman followed in his father's footsteps, becoming an accountant and tax preparer, in a practice that specializes in working with professional athletes from all corners of the sporting world. Rothman married his childhood sweetheart, Myrna, and they have four children and six grandchildren. While their children were growing up, it was not unusual for a client-player to be seated around the Rothman family dinner table. In recent years, metal detecting has become Rothman's favorite pastime. His desire to share his experiences with as many people as possible was the driving force behind this book.

CPSIA information can be obtained at www.ICGtesting.com
Printed in the USA
BVOW02s0026060815

412077BV00001B/1/P